CONSTRUCTION 123

Alaina Downing

Construction 123

ISBN: 979-8-9957605-0-4

Printed in the United States of America

Boone Boys Publishing
Columbia, MO

To my boys, Knox and Noah— thank you for making the ordinary so much fun! I love being your mom and going on our many adventures.

To my husband, my best friend, Colton— thank you for supporting me with every idea I surprise you with. You inspire me to try new things. I truly couldn't do this life without you.

The construction site is my favorite place to be!

Will you count 1 to 10 with me?

1 big excavator digging in the ground.

2 buckets on the backhoe moving up and down.

3
loud dump trucks removing dirt from the site.

4 busy workers building
it just right.

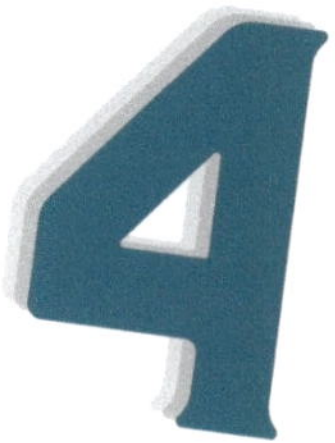

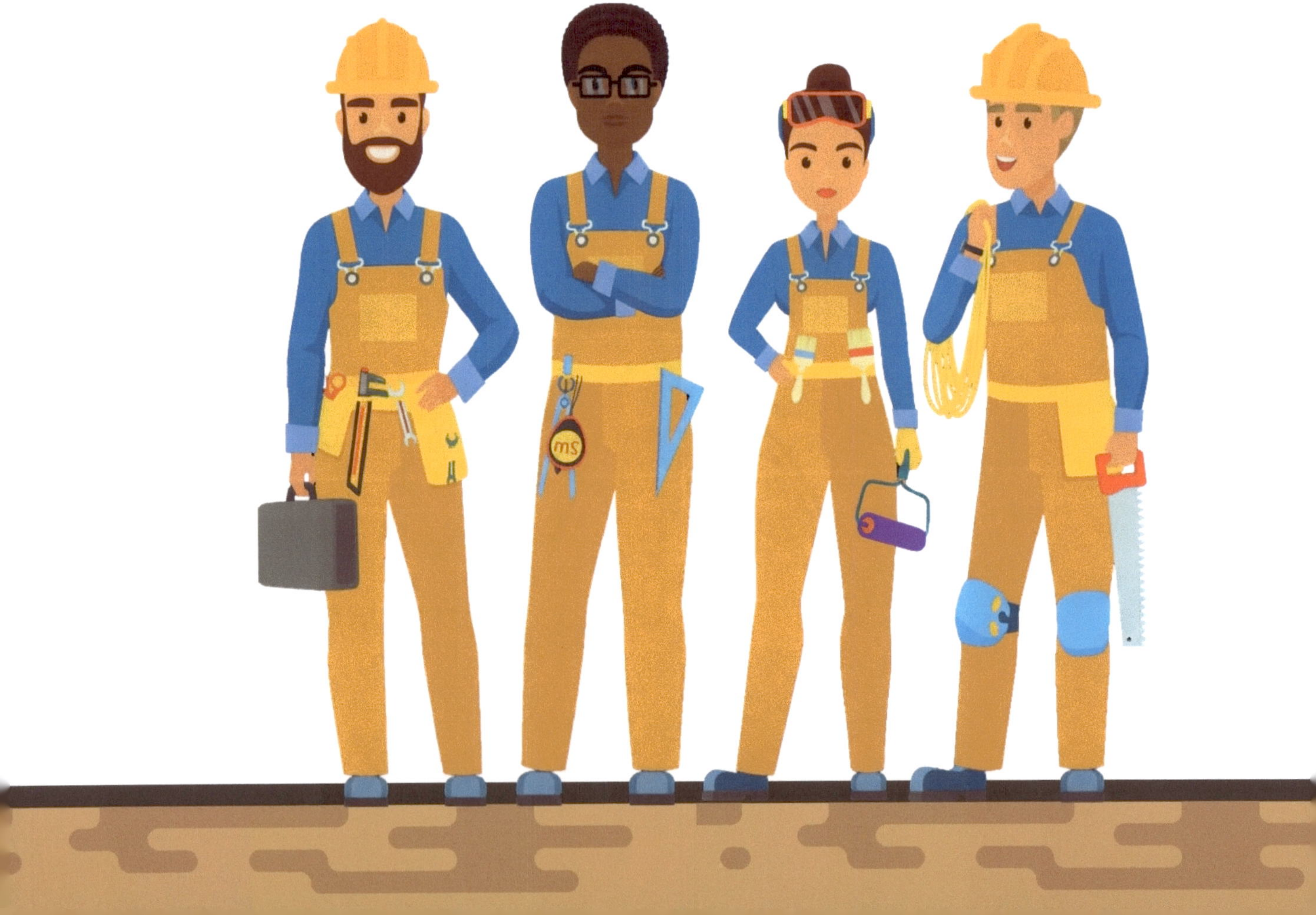

5 cement mixers pour cement where it should.

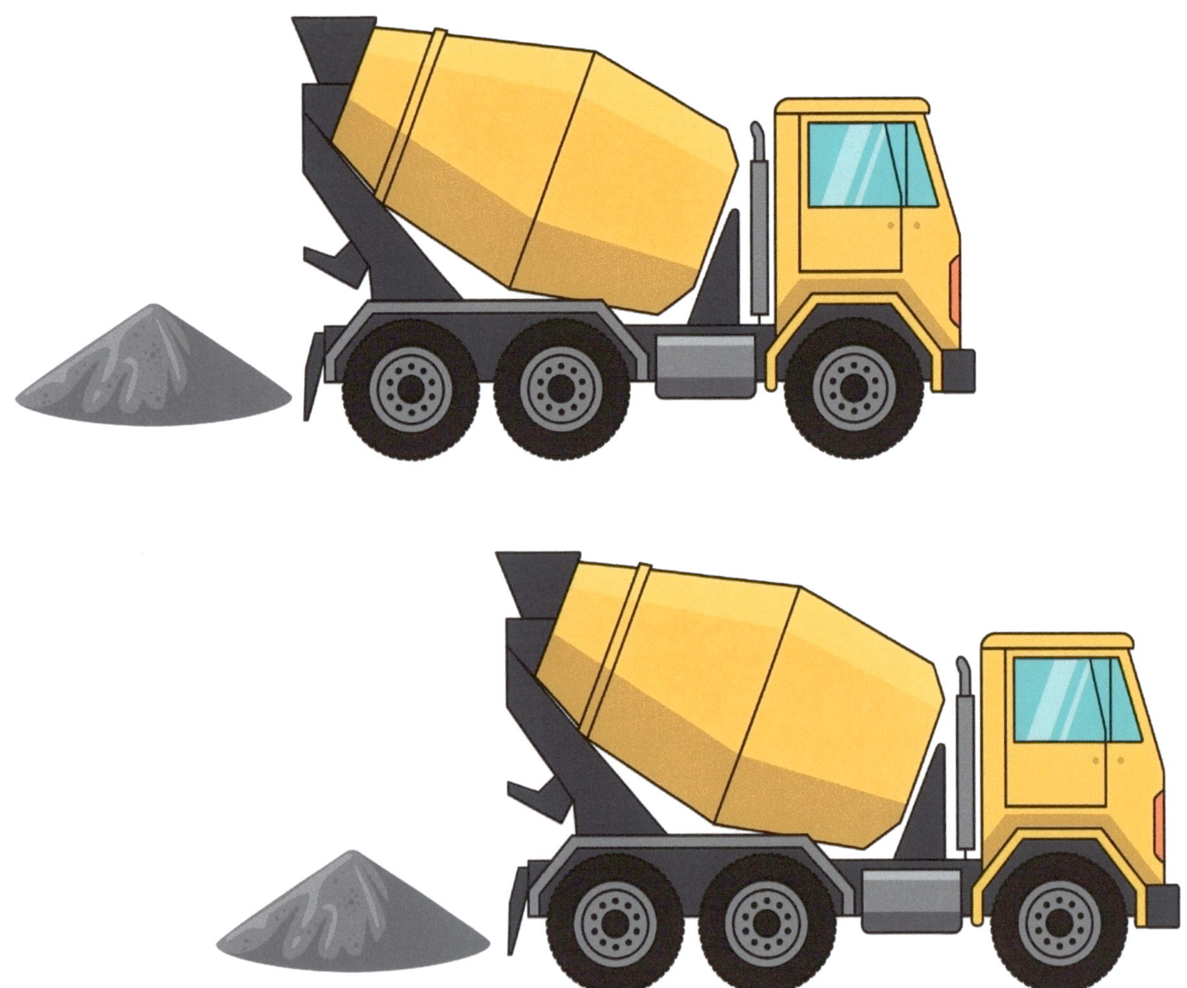

6

shiny nails get
hammered into wood.

7 piles of rocks piled way up high.

8 2x4s to be cut – oh my!

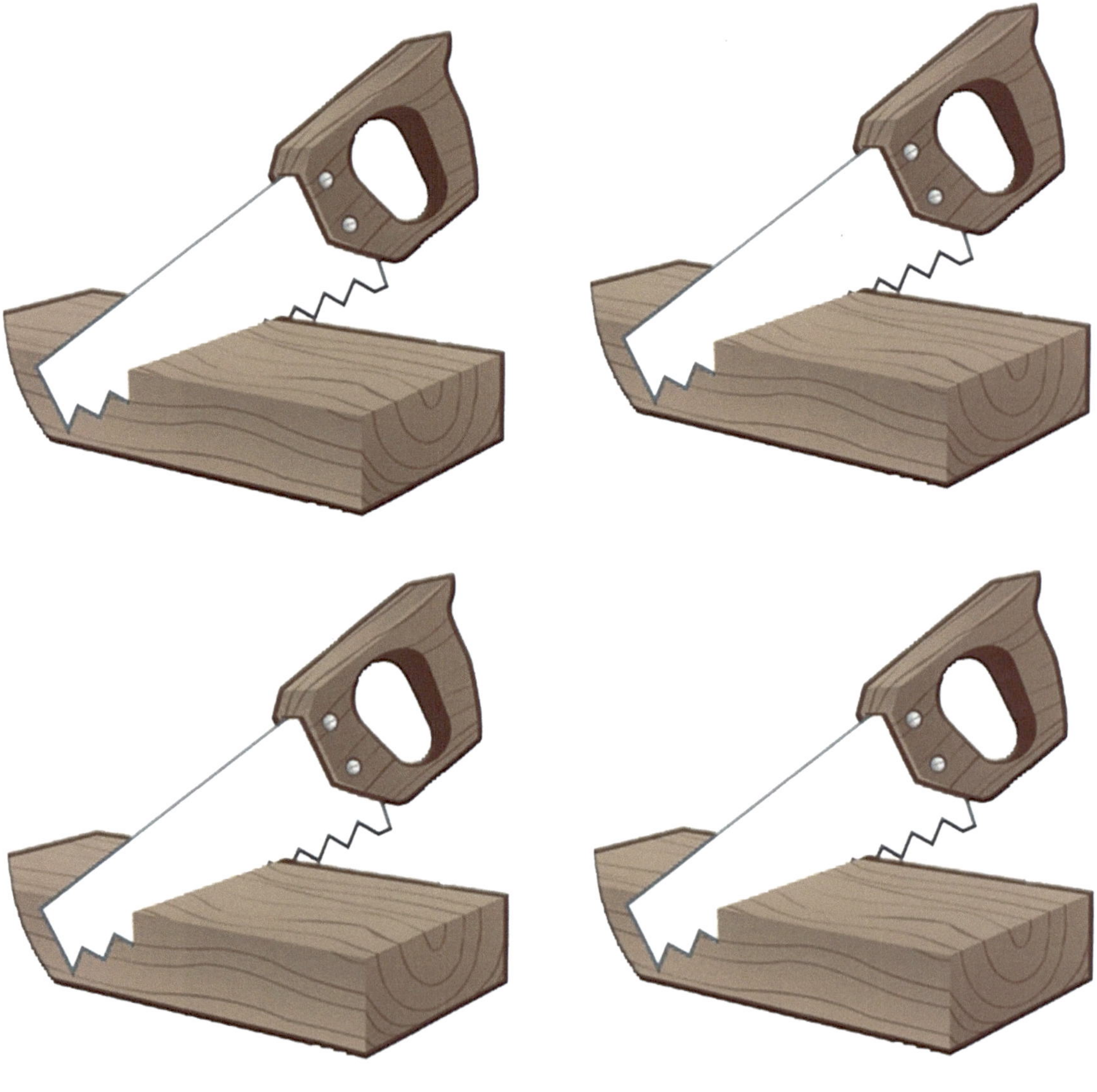

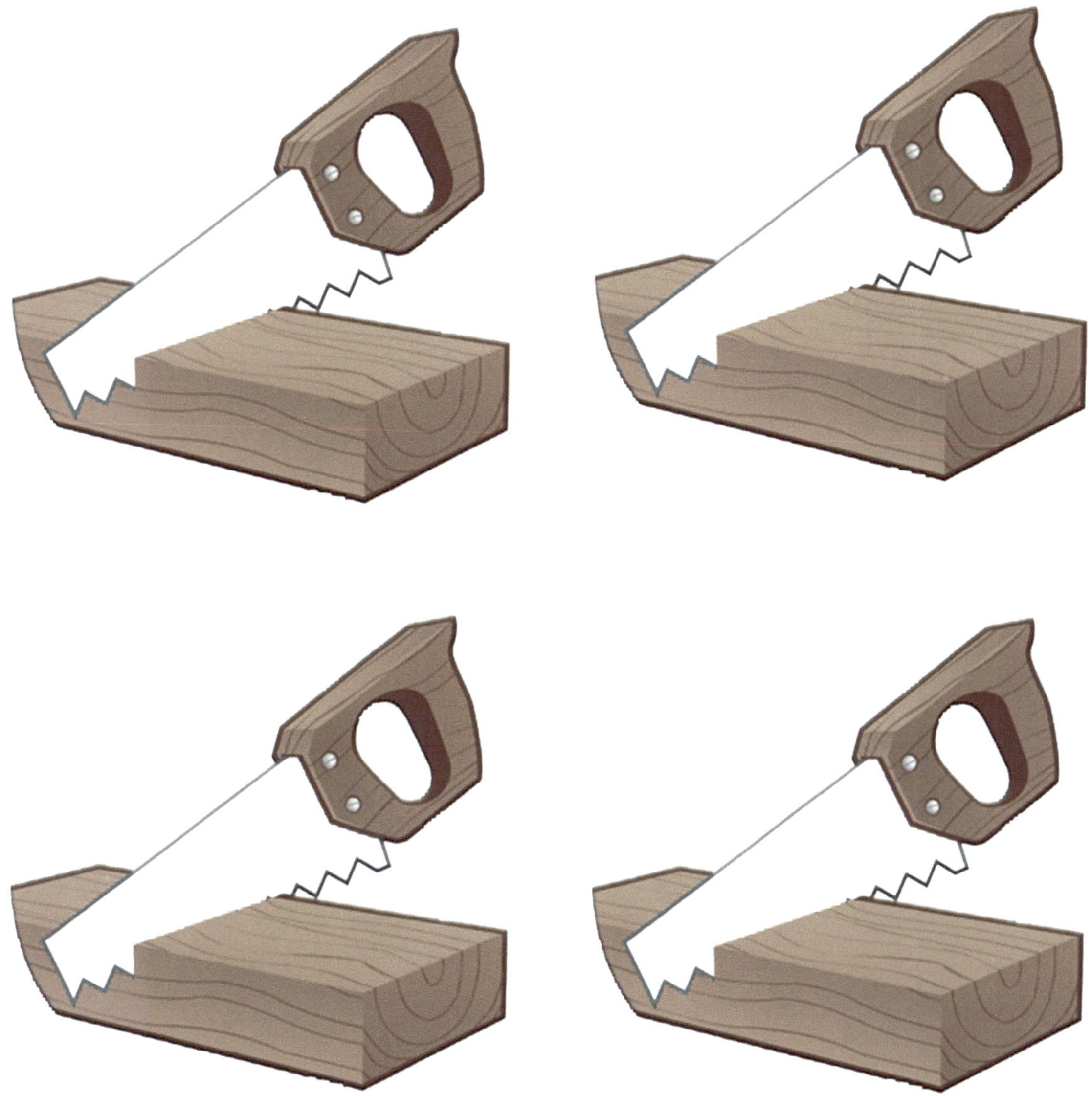

9 thwacks of the hammer I hear on repeat.

10 hours of work done – it's time to take a seat!